Copyright © 2024 by Erin Herald

All rights reserved.

No portion of this book may be reproduced in any form without written permission from the publisher or author, except as permitted by U.S. copyright law.

Bible Stories for Little Believers

by Erin Herald

Dedicated to James and Simon, never let your lights be dimmed

The story of the Bible reads
how creation came to be

It tells us truths from long ago
and how our Jesus loves us so

Signs and miracles galore
show the love of the God we adore

Noah is a good place to start
when God told him to build an ark

And though the people teased and poked
Noah listened and built that boat

The animals came, 2 by 2
some came by land, and others flew

Soon floods rained but the animals were safe for the next 40 days the flood waters came

After that time Noah saw a white bird
a dove, in its beak with a leaf was a word

The floods had ceased and the
waters receded
God's new creation was now
completed

A rainbow was seen in the sky that day
a sign that a promise from God was made

Never again would he send flood waters proving the love of our good, good Father

Another story that's worth a mention
Moses and Pharoah now have the attention

Though born to a Hebrew,
Moses lived with a crown
until he decided to set royalty down

He demanded freedom for his people from Pharoah
but Pharaoh ignored his plea to let go

God sent the plagues -
frogs, bugs, and rains -

But when Pharaoh's son died
he finally caved

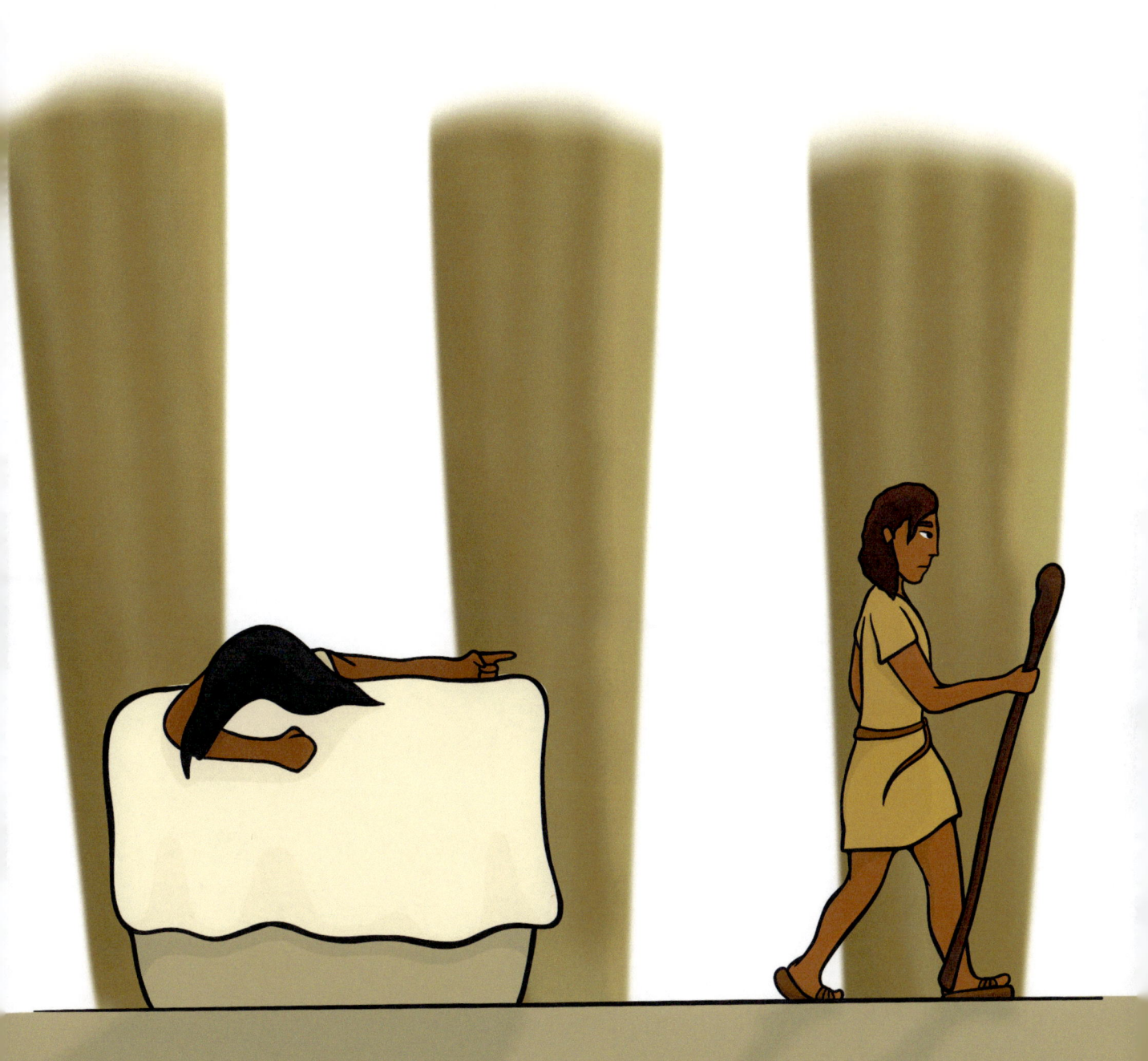

Moses then led his people through the desert
then Pharaoh decided his power he'd assert

He gathered an army to chase down the Hebrews
little did he know he sorely would lose

Moses and his people came to the Red Sea when there was no path, God said to trust me

And with Moses' staff the Red Sea parted through walls of water,
the freed people started

Right on their heels came the Pharaoh
a mighty army with chariots bellowed

But when they reached the part in the sea
and God's people already got across clean

Down came the water on chariots
and Pharoah

for God freed His people,
and free they will go

Another good story is David and Goliath
a small shepherd boy who defeated a giant

The Israelites cowered inside of their tents
while Goliath stood there with no offense

Then David arrived with God on his side
and he had a sling, 3 smooth stones inside

He swung his sling and the stone hit Goliath a direct hit to the head and down goes the giant

So David won the battle with just rocks and a sling
the same David who would one day be king

Speaking of David who one day would reign
so would another, by a different name

His name was Jesus, born to mother Mary
He came to save the poor, the lame,
and extraordinary

His 33 years on Earth would consist of feeding 5000 from some bread and some fish

He performed miracles, like healing the lame
the entire nation soon knew His name

Some of them loved Him, and some refused the Romans feared a revolt of the Jews

Soon enough they took Him and arrested our Savior
they hurt and forced Him to the cross a bit later

As Jesus died the Earth would tremble it would be a day they all would remember

In a tomb Jesus lay, in a grave for 3 days then death was defeated, and in Him was the way

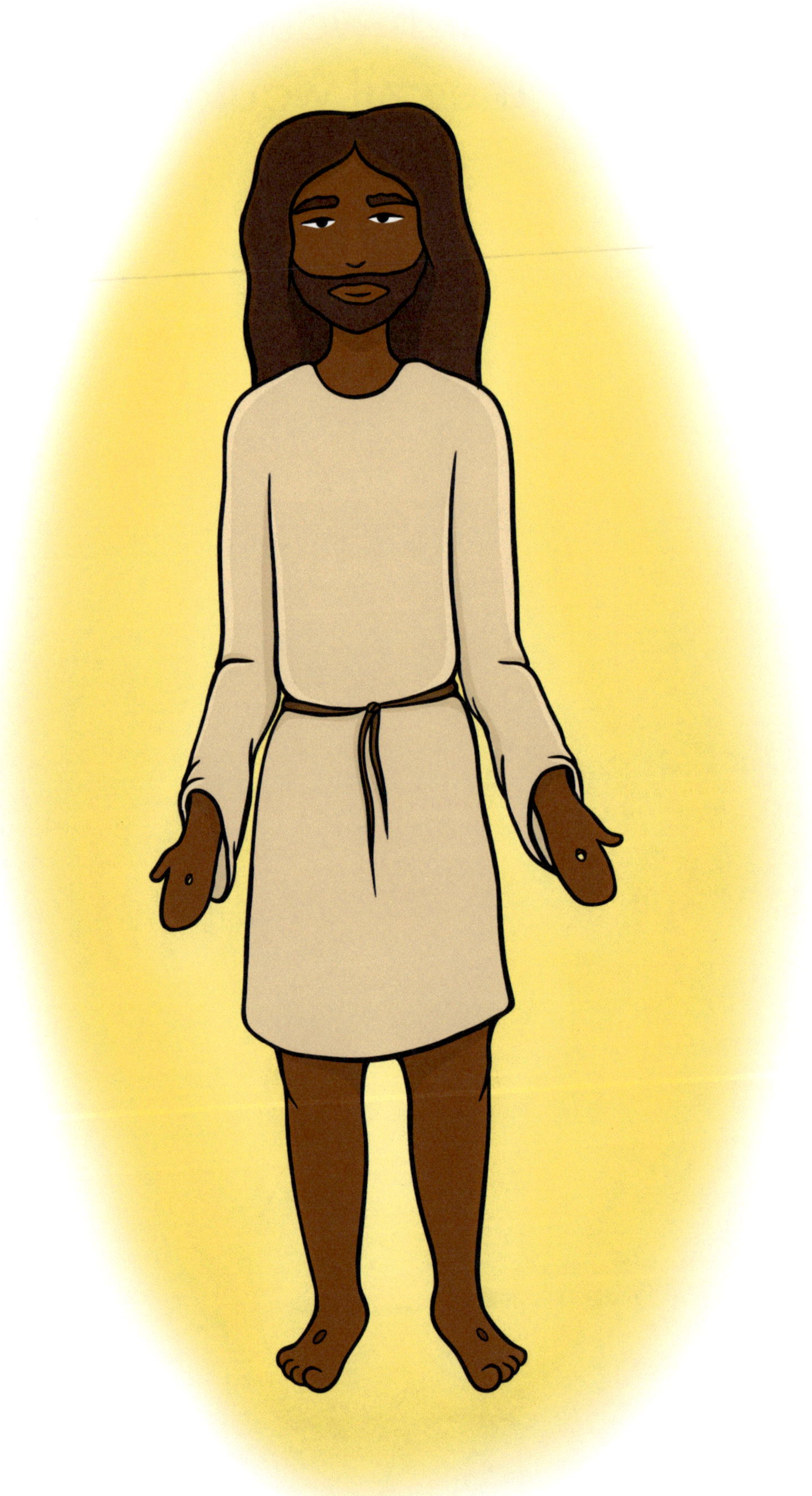

Jesus went through so much hurt just so we don't return to dirt

He saved us from our sin and shame on Himself he took the blame

Now He sits with God on a throne In Heaven, waiting for us to come home

Made in the USA
Columbia, SC
06 November 2024